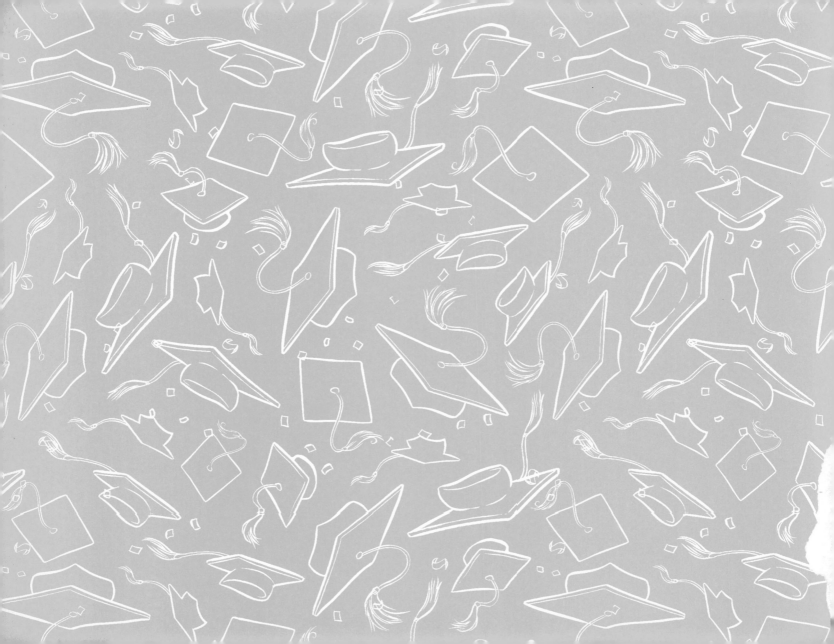

BRING IT!

A LITTLE "BAGGAGE" TO HELP
THE HIGH SCHOOL GRADUATE CARRY ON

by Tom Hegg

illustrated by Lindsay Nohl, Chris Hajny
and Francesca Buchko

TRISTAN PUBLISHING

MINNEAPOLIS

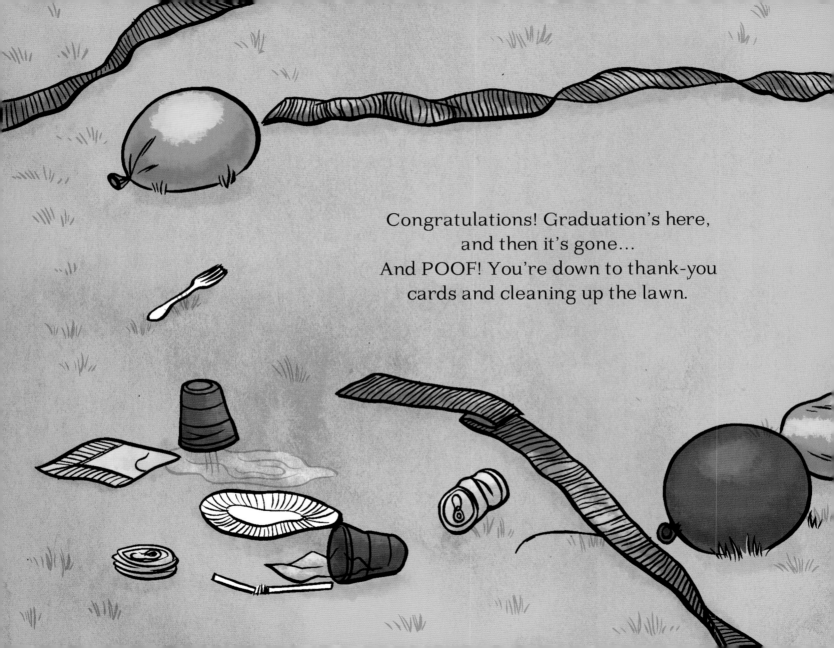

Congratulations! Graduation's here,
and then it's gone...
And POOF! You're down to thank-you
cards and cleaning up the lawn.

The locker's long since emptied out...
it all got hauled back home,
And now, your room is looking kind
of like the Fall of Rome.

The gee-gaws, doo-dads, dealy-bobs
　　and junk are piled so high,
You wish that they would disappear,
　　and really don't know why.

Relax. There's time to sort it out. Not lots, but still, enough…
Besides, when all is said and done, it's just a bunch of stuff.

And stuff is secondary when you're making up your mind
About the things to bring along, and those to leave behind.

So this is the "Commencement" part:
A whole new life in store…
And much of it depends upon what
makes it out that door.

The most important things to bring
don't take up any space.
They're not among the knick-knacks
that have overwhelmed the place.

They dwell within your memory, and deep inside your heart…
And bringing them to mind right now might be a place to start.

There's personal integrity, and all you've learned and heard
About your conscience, character, your honor and your word.

ORBITING

They say "nobody's perfect." That might be. But even so,
You bring enough integrity and hey – you never know…

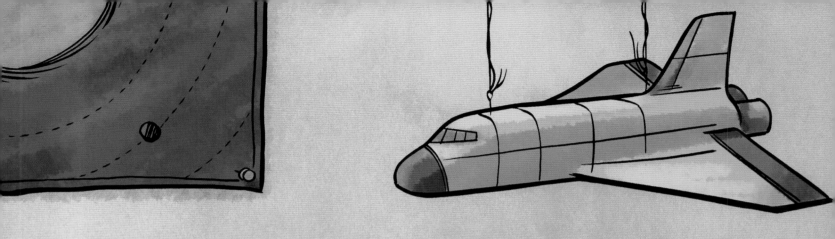

Get rid of those bad habits, while you're bidding things goodbye.
Declare your independence, spread your wings, and off you fly!

Bring pride in who and whose you are,
and seek to understand.
Be slow to come to judgment, and be
swift to lend a hand.

Dispose of arrogance – do
not recycle! Place within
A sharps container, well
away from unprotected skin.

 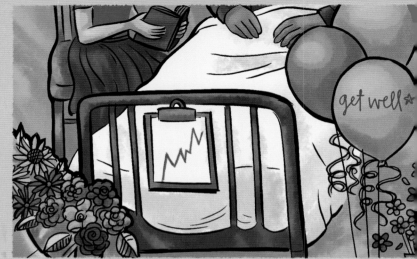

I hope you bring some guilt… but not immobilizing shame.
I mean the guilt that helps you do for those who'd do the same.

The guilt that moves you when you hear that there are mouths to feed.
The guilt that gets you off the couch and out to those in need.

Be sure to bring proportion and perspective when you do.
You have a lot to give, but there are limitations, too.

Bring curiosity! No way to take too much of that...
(Except the dangerous variety that killed the cat.)

I mean the curiosity that floated a balloon...
Then took us off to Kitty Hawk, and right on to the moon.

The curiosity that gave us even the control
To see our DNA – the very threshold of the soul.

The kind of curiosity that just might save us all...
And gosh, that would be nice of you... so, Bring It! Have a ball!

Be sure to take your common sense... and here, I must insist.
It's really not an option, and I trust you won't resist.

Of course, there are necessities that you can always use...
A bar of soap, a toothbrush, maybe clothing and some shoes...

A little money helps a lot – be careful – not too much.
Don't lend, and get a reputation as an easy touch!

Go on and bring your squishy pillow
and your teddy bear.
Your roommate's bound to bring
them too, so no one's going to care.

But most of all, you bring yourself.
In each and every way.
Be present. Listen. See. Taste.
Touch. Smell. Each and every day.

Please know that you are loved by
those of us you leave behind.
We pray that you will also have the
love you've dreamed to find.

And may the One who loves us all be always at your side,
To shield you and protect you as your guardian and guide,

Above you to watch over you, on stormy days and fair,
Below you to support you, in your trials and despair,

Behind you to deliver you from dangers near and far,
Within you to inspire you, in all the things you are.

And may these blessings follow you, beyond that open door,
Today, and every day, until that day... and evermore.

For Peggy.
L,
M

Hegg, Tom.
  Bring it! / written by Tom Hegg.
    p. cm.
  ISBN 978-0-931674-58-7 (hardcover : alk. paper)
  I. Title.
  PS3558.E4175B75 2012
  811'.54--dc22

                    2011018061

                 TRISTAN Publishing, Inc.
                2355 Louisiana Avenue North
                 Golden Valley, MN 55427

Text copyright © 2012, Tom Hegg
Illustrations copyright © 2012, TRISTAN Publishing, Inc.
ISBN 978-0-931674-58-7
Printed in China
First Printing

To learn about all of our **books with a message** please visit
www.TRISTANpublishing.com

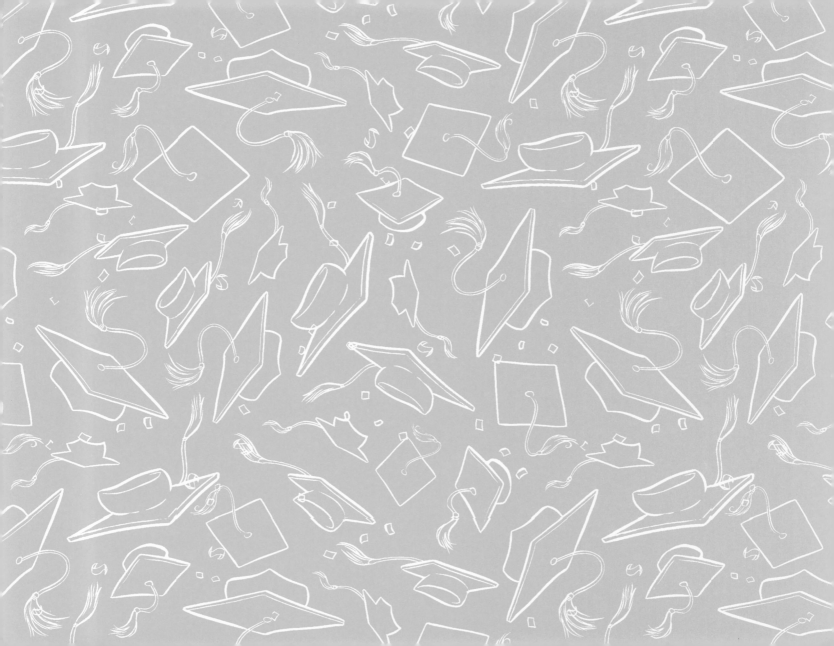

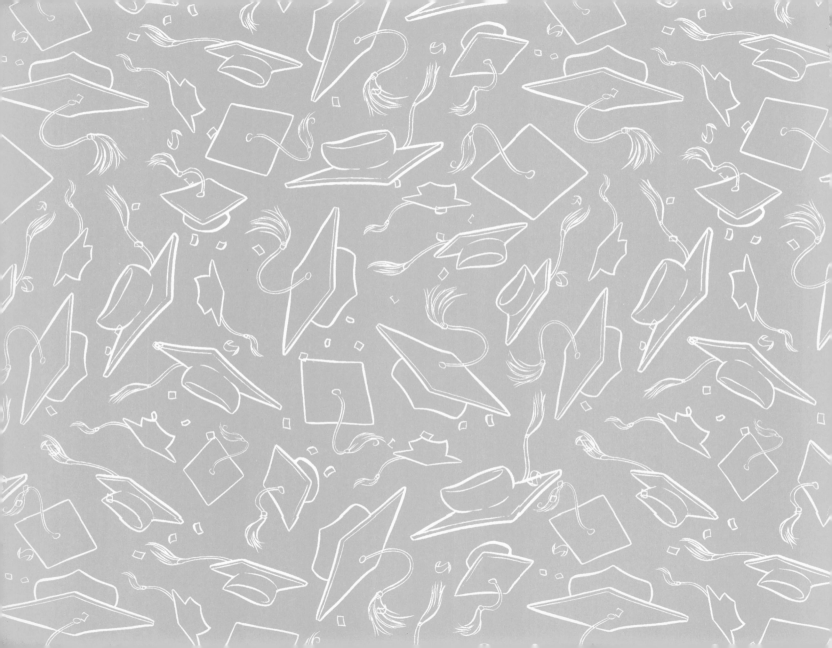